Ninja Foodi Cookbook

Easy and Delicious Recipes for Indoor Grilling and Air Frying Perfection

Kenzie Zimmerman

© Copyright 2020 by Kenzie Zimmerman - All rights reserved.

The following Book is reproduced below with the goal of providing information that is as accurate and reliable as possible. Regardless, purchasing this Book can be seen as consent to the fact that both the publisher and the author of this book are in no way experts on the topics discussed within and that any recommendations or suggestions that are made herein are for entertainment purposes only. Professionals should be consulted as needed prior to undertaking any of the action endorsed herein.

This declaration is deemed fair and valid by both the American Bar Association and the Committee of Publishers Association and is legally binding throughout the United States.

Furthermore, the transmission, duplication, or reproduction of any of the following work including specific information will be considered an illegal act irrespective of if it is done electronically or in print. This extends to creating a secondary or tertiary copy of the work or a recorded copy and is only allowed with the express written consent from the Publisher. All additional right reserved.

The information in the following pages is broadly considered a truthful and accurate account of facts and as such, any inattention, use, or misuse of the information in question by the reader will render any resulting actions solely under their purview. There are no scenarios in which the publisher or the original author of this work can be in any fashion deemed liable for any hardship or damages that may befall them after undertaking information described herein.

Additionally, the information in the following pages is intended only for informational purposes and should thus be thought of as universal. As befitting its nature, it is presented without assurance regarding its prolonged validity or interim quality. Trademarks that are mentioned are done without written consent and can in no way be considered an endorsement from the trademark holder.

TABLE OF CONTENTS

INTRODUCTION 7

WHAT IS THE TENDER CRISP TECHNOLOGY? 7
HOW TO USE THE NINJA FOODI? 7

BREAKFAST RECIPES 10

HOMEMADE YOGURT 11
HARD-BOILED EGGS 13
EASY CHEESY EGG BAKE 15
CRISPY BACON HASH AND BAKED EGGS 17
UPSIDE-DOWN BROCCOLI AND CHEESE QUICHE 19
SIMPLE STRAWBERRY JAM 21
APPLE-CRANBERRY OATMEAL 23

APPETIZERS AND SNACKS 25

WATERMELON JERKY 26
DRIED MANGO 28
BEET CHIPS 29
MAPLE CANDIED BACON 30
CHILI-RANCH CHICKEN WINGS 32
CRISPY CHEESY ARANCINI 34
BUFFALO CHICKEN MEATBALLS 37
LOADED SMASHED POTATOES 39
FRIED PICKLES 41

MEAT RECIPES 44

CHICKEN ALFREDO APPLES 45
BAKED SOY CHICKEN 47
SALSA COCONUT CHICKEN 49
CHICKEN COCONUT CURRY 51
CHICKEN PAILLARDS WITH FRESH TOMATO SAUCE 53
KOREAN CHILI PORK 55
KOREAN PORK 57
GARLIC BUTTER PORK 59
BOURBON BARBECUE—GLAZED PORK CHOPS 61
ROAST BEEF WITH GARLIC 63
GRILLED STEAK & POTATOES 65
AUTHENTIC KOREAN FLANK STEAK 67
GRILLED BEEF BURGERS 69
MIDDLE EASTERN LAMB STEW 71
CHORIZO CASHEW SOUP 73

Bacon Potato Salad 75

FISH AND SEAFOOD RECIPES 77

Cedar-Plank Salmon 78
Grilled Coconut Shrimp with Shishito Peppers 80
Clams with Spicy Tomato Broth and Garlic Mayo 82
Grilled Swordfish with Tomatoes and Oregano 85
Grilled Spiced Snapper with Mango and Red Onion Salad 87
Grilled Shrimp, Zucchini, and Tomatoes with Feta 89

VEGETARIAN RECIPES 91

Penne with Mushrooms and Gruyère 92
Easy Eggplant Parmesan 94
Mediterranean White Bean Salad 96
Cajun Twice-Baked Potatoes 99
"Spanish" Rice and Beans 102

DESSERT RECIPES 104

Blueberry Lemon Muffins 105
Grilled Pound Cake with Berry Compote 107
Sweet Cream Cheese Wontons 109
Air Fryer Cinnamon Rolls 111
Smoked Apple Crumble 113
Bread Pudding with Cranberry 115
Black and White Brownies 117

CONCLUSION 119

Introduction

What is the Tender Crisp Technology?

Cooking tougher ingredients or meats with pressure cooking makes them into much tender and delicious food. On the other hand, air frying makes our food crispier and have a tasty crust in it. The combo of both air frying and pressure cooking is the basic working principle of Ninja Foodi and is called the Tender Crisp Technology. It creates a perfect tender and juicy food that is crispy on its outer surface. The cooking procedures initiate with pressure cooking, followed by a customized air frying standard to achieve the crispiness of your choice.

Tender Crisp Technology utilizes steam (super-heated) to infuse both flavor and moisture faster into the food cooked with pressure cooking. Afterward, the crisping lid blows down hot air to every corner of your food, and makes it crispier and finishes it with a certain golden color that can't be achieved by any other cooking appliance.

How to use the Ninja Foodi?

The food with the Ninja Foodi is the best both a pressure cooker and air fryer can give you, but this time it's going to be in a single pot. You can prepare wholesome food with multi-texture 360 meals by preparing vegetables, grains, and proteins in a single go.

Modern electric pressure cookers can help you simplify everyday food preparation; therefore, learning to use Ninja Foodi can be both beneficial and fun! It may sound like a fancy electric pressure cooker, but your Ninja Foodi takes it even further with its awesome capabilities. While Ninja Foodi has the basic pressure cooker function, it can also air and steam fry your food and bake it using unique heating elements.

Generally, the Ninja Foodi consists of a 6.5-quart removable cooking pot, Cook & Crisp Basket, a pressure lid, and a crisping lid. When it comes to its most important parts and accessories, it is equipped with handles, pressure release valve, red float valve, silicone ring, reversible rack, detachable diffuser, heat shield, cooker base, anti-clog cap, air outlet vent, condensation collector, power cord, and sensor. Accessories that are sold separately include Cook & Crisp™ layered insert, loaf pan, crisper pan, multi-purpose pan, roasting rack insert, and dehydrating rack.

Your Ninja Foodi also has built-in multiple safety features. However, always use caution when opening the lid; never place your face and hands over the unit and use heat-resistant oven mitts.

You will have an electric pressure cooker and air fryer in one! It has two lids, which allow you to pressure cook and crisp in the same cooking pot. Use a pressure lid with functions such as pressure cook, slow cook, and steam. Use a crisping lid with functions such as air crisp, broil, bake, and roast. Use the "SEAR/SAUTE" function with an open lid.

That being said, this particular book has been designed to help beginners get a grip on the appliance, and keeping that in mind, the first chapter of the book covers all the basic information that you might need to know regarding the Ninja Foodi Grill.

So, what are you waiting for? Jump right in and start exploring!

Breakfast Recipes

Homemade Yogurt

Preparation Time: 15 minutes

Cooking Time: 12 Hours

Servings: 8

Ingredients:
- ½ gallon whole milk
- 2 tablespoons plain yogurt with active live cultures
- 1 tablespoon vanilla extract (optional)
- ½ cup honey (optional)

Directions:
1. Pour the milk into the pot. Assemble the Pressure Lid, making sure the pressure release valve is in the Vent position. Select Sear/Sauté and set it to Medium. Select Start/Stop to begin.
2. Bring the milk to 180°F, checking the temperature often and stirring frequently so the milk does not burn at the bottom. Select Start/Stop to turn off Sear/Sauté.
3. Allow the milk to cool to 110°F, continuing to check the temperature often and stirring frequently. Gently skim off the "skin" on the milk and discard.
4. Stir in the yogurt and whisk until incorporated.

5. Assemble the Pressure Lid, making sure the pressure release valve is in the Vent position. Let incubate for 8 hours.

6. After 8 hours, transfer the yogurt to a glass container and chill for 4 hours in the refrigerator.

7. Add the vanilla and honey (if using) to the yogurt and mix until well combined. Cover and place the glass bowl back in the refrigerator or divide the yogurt among airtight glass jars.

TIP: If you prefer a thicker Greek-style yogurt, let the yogurt strain through cheesecloth into a large mixing bowl overnight in the refrigerator.

Nutrition: Calories: 149; Total fat: 8g; Saturated fat: 5g; Cholesterol: 25mg; Sodium: 99mg; Carbohydrates: 13g; Fiber: 0g; Protein: 8g

Hard-Boiled Eggs

Preparation Time: 2 minutes

Cooking Time: 15 Minutes

Servings: 2-12 eggs

Ingredients:
- 1 cup of water
- 2 to 12 eggs

Directions:
1. Place the Reversible Rack in the pot in the lower position. Add the water and arrange the eggs on the rack in a single layer.

2. Assemble the Pressure Lid, making sure the pressure release valve is in the Seal position. Select Pressure and set to Low. Set the time to 8 minutes. Select Start/Stop to begin.

3. While the eggs are cooking, prepare a large bowl of ice water.

4. When pressure cooking is complete, quick release the pressure by moving the pressure release valve to the Vent position. Carefully remove the lid when the unit has finished releasing pressure.

5. Using a slotted spoon, immediately transfer the eggs to the ice water bath and allow to cool for 5 minutes.

TIP: Hard-boiled eggs with hard yolks are ideal for deviled eggs, but if you prefer runny yolks, then you will want soft-boiled eggs. For soft-boiled eggs, cook on Low for 2 to 3 minutes, and for medium-boiled eggs, cook on Low for 5 to 6 minutes.

Nutrition: (1 egg) Calories: 71; Total fat: 5g; Saturated fat: 2g; Cholesterol: 211mg; Sodium: 70mg; Carbohydrates: 0g; Fiber: 0g; Protein: 6g

Easy Cheesy Egg Bake

Preparation Time: 5 minutes

Cooking Time: 27 Minutes

Servings: 4

Ingredients:

- 4 eggs
- 1 cup milk
- 1 teaspoon sea salt
- 1 teaspoon freshly ground black pepper
- 1 cup shredded Cheddar cheese
- 1 red bell pepper, seeded and chopped
- 8 ounces ham, chopped
- 1 cup of water

Directions:

1. In a medium mixing bowl, whisk together the eggs, milk, salt, and black pepper. Stir in the Cheddar cheese.
2. Place the bell pepper and ham in the Multi-Purpose Pan or an 8-inch baking pan. Pour the egg mixture over the pepper and ham. Cover the pan with aluminum foil and place it on the Reversible Rack.
3. Pour the water into the pot. Place the rack with the pan in the pot in the lower position.

4. Assemble the Pressure Lid, making sure the pressure release valve is in the Seal position. Select Pressure and set to High. Set the time to 20 minutes. Select Start/Stop to begin.

5. When pressure cooking is complete, quick release the pressure by moving the pressure release valve to the Vent position. Carefully remove the lid when the unit has finished releasing pressure.

6. When cooking is complete, remove the pan from the pot and place it on a cooling rack. Let cool for 5 minutes, then serve.

TIP: Swap the red bell pepper for other veggies like broccoli, spinach, and onions, but stay away from those that will release water, like tomatoes, zucchini, and mushrooms. Chicken and smoked sausage make good substitutes for the ham.

Nutrition: Calories: 332; Total fat: 21g; Saturated fat: 10g; Cholesterol: 280mg; Sodium: 1693mg; Carbohydrates: 6g; Fiber: 1g; Protein: 28g

Crispy Bacon Hash and Baked Eggs

Preparation Time: 10 minutes

Cooking Time: 40 Minutes

Servings: 4

Ingredients:
- 6 slices bacon, chopped
- 1 yellow onion, diced
- 2 russet potatoes, peeled and diced
- 1 teaspoon paprika
- 1 teaspoon sea salt
- 1 teaspoon freshly ground black pepper
- 1 teaspoon garlic salt
- 4 eggs

Directions:

1. Select Sear/Sauté and set it to Medium-High. Select Start/Stop to begin. Allow the pot to preheat for 5 minutes.

2. Once hot, add the bacon to the pot. Cook, stirring occasionally, for 5 minutes, or until the bacon is crispy.

3. Add the onion and potatoes to the pot. Sprinkle with paprika, sea salt, pepper, and garlic salt.

4. Close the Crisping Lid. Select Bake/Roast, set the temperature to 350°F, and set the time to 25 minutes. Cook, stirring occasionally until the potatoes are tender and golden brown.

5. Crack the eggs onto the surface of the hash. Close the Crisping Lid. Select Bake/Roast, set the temperature to 350°F, and set the time to 10 minutes.

6. Check the eggs after 3 minutes. Continue cooking for the remaining 7 minutes, checking occasionally, until your desired doneness is achieved. Serve immediately.

Nutrition: Calories: 364; Total fat: 24g; Saturated fat: 8g; Cholesterol: 240mg; Sodium: 1008mg; Carbohydrates: 24g; Fiber: 2g; Protein: 14g

Upside-Down Broccoli and Cheese Quiche

Preparation Time: 10 minutes
Cooking Time: 20 Minutes
Servings: 6

Ingredients:
- 8 eggs
- ½ cup milk
- 1 teaspoon sea salt
- 1 teaspoon freshly ground black pepper
- 1 cup shredded Cheddar cheese
- 1 tablespoon extra-virgin olive oil
- 1 yellow onion, chopped
- 2 garlic cloves, minced
- 2 cups thinly sliced broccoli florets
- 1 refrigerated piecrust, at room temperature

Directions:
1. Select Sear/Sauté and set to High. Select Start/Stop it to begin. Allow the pot to preheat for 5 minutes.
2. In a large mixing bowl, whisk together the eggs, milk, salt, and pepper. Stir in the Cheddar cheese.

3. Put the oil, onion, and garlic in the preheated pot and stir occasionally for 5 minutes. Add the broccoli florets and sauté for another 5 minutes.

4. Pour the egg mixture over the vegetables and gently stir for 1 minute (this will allow the egg mixture to temper well and ensure that it cooks evenly under the crust).

5. Lay the piecrust evenly on top of the filling mixture, folding over the edges if necessary. Make a small cut in the center of the piecrust so that steam can escape during baking.

6. Close the Crisping Lid. Select Broil and set the time to 10 minutes. Select Start/Stop to begin.

7. When cooking is complete, remove the pot and place it on a heat-resistant surface. Let the quiche rest for 5 to 10 minutes before serving.

Nutrition: Calories: 393; Total fat: 26g; Saturated fat: 10g; Cholesterol: 304mg; Sodium: 773mg; Carbohydrates: 26g; Fiber: 2g; Protein: 16g

Simple Strawberry Jam

Preparation Time: 10 minutes

Cooking Time: 42 Minutes

Servings: 1 ½ Cups

Ingredients:
- 2 pounds strawberries, hulled and halved
- Juice of 2 lemons
- 1½ cups granulated sugar

Directions:
1. Place the strawberries, lemon juice, and sugar in the pot. Using a silicone potato masher, mash the ingredients together to begin to release the strawberry juices.
2. Assemble the Pressure Lid, making sure the pressure release valve is in the Seal position. Select Pressure and

set to High. Set the time to 1 minute. Select Start/Stop to begin.

3. When pressure cooking is complete, allow the pressure to naturally release for 10 minutes, then quickly release any remaining pressure by moving the pressure release valve to the Vent position. Carefully remove the lid when the pressure has finished releasing.

4. Select Sear/Sauté and set it to Medium-High. Select Start/Stop to begin. Allow the jam to reduce for 20 minutes, or until it tightens.

5. Mash the strawberries using the silicone potato masher for a textured jam, or transfer the strawberry mixture to a food processor and purée for a smooth consistency. Let the jam cool, pour it into a glass jar, and refrigerate for up to 2 weeks.

TIP: This natural jam may be a bit looser than store-bought versions because it uses all whole ingredients. If you prefer to thicken the jam, stir in flavorless gelatin after step 4.

Nutrition: (1 tablespoon) Calories: 23; Total fat: 0g; Saturated fat: 0g; Cholesterol: 0mg; Sodium: 0mg; Carbohydrates: 6g; Fiber: 0g; Protein: 0g

Apple-Cranberry Oatmeal

Preparation Time: 5 minutes

Cooking Time: 27 Minutes

Servings: 4

Ingredients:

- 2 cups gluten-free steel-cut oats
- 3¾ cups water
- ¼ cup apple cider vinegar
- 1 tablespoon ground cinnamon
- ½ teaspoon ground nutmeg
- ½ teaspoon vanilla extract
- ½ cup dried cranberries, plus more for garnish
- 2 apples, peeled, cored, and diced
- 1/8 teaspoon sea salt
- Maple syrup, for topping

Directions:

1. Add the oats, water, vinegar, cinnamon, nutmeg, vanilla, cranberries, apples, and salt to the pot. Assemble the Pressure Lid, making sure the pressure release valve is in the Seal position. Select Pressure and set to High. Set the time to 11 minutes. Select Start/Stop to begin.
2. When pressure cooking is complete, allow the pressure to naturally release for 10 minutes, then quickly release any remaining pressure by moving the pressure release

valve to the Vent position. Carefully remove the lid when the pressure has finished releasing.

3. Stir the oatmeal and serve immediately. Top with maple syrup and more dried cranberries, as desired.

TIP: If you prefer old-fashioned oats, you can substitute an equal amount of them for the steel-cut oats and reduce pressure Cooking Time to 6 minutes. You can also add more water if you prefer thinner oatmeal.

Nutrition: Calories: 399; Total fat: 6g; Saturated fat: 1g; Cholesterol: 0mg; Sodium: 76mg; Carbohydrates: 71g; Fiber: 12g; Protein: 14g

Appetizers and Snacks

Watermelon Jerky

Preparation Time: 5 minutes

Cooking Time: 12 Hours

Servings: ½ Cup

Ingredients:

- 1 cup seedless watermelon (1-inch) cubes

Directions:

1. Arrange the watermelon cubes in a single layer in the Cook & Crisp Basket. Place the basket in the pot and close the Crisping Lid.
2. Press Dehydrate, set the temperature to 135°F and set the time to 12 hours. Select Start/Stop to begin.

3. When dehydrating is complete, remove the basket from the pot and transfer the jerky to an airtight container.

Nutrition Calories: 46; Total fat: 0g; Saturated fat: 0g; Cholesterol: 0mg; Sodium: 6mg; Carbohydrates: 12g; Fiber: 1g; Protein: 1g

Dried Mango

Preparation Time: 5 minutes

Cooking Time: 8 Hours

Servings: 2

Ingredients:

- ½ mango, peeled, pitted, and cut into 3/8-inch slices

Directions:

1. Arrange the mango slices flat in a single layer in the Cook & Crisp Basket. Place in the pot and close the Crisping Lid.
2. Press Dehydrate, set the temperature to 135°F and set the time to 8 hours. Select Start/Stop to begin.
3. When dehydrating is complete, remove the basket from the pot and transfer the mango slices to an airtight container.

Nutrition Calories: 67; Total fat: 0g; Saturated fat: 0g; Cholesterol: 0mg; Sodium: 2mg; Carbohydrates: 18g; Fiber: 2g; Protein: 1g

Beet Chips

Preparation Time: 5 minutes

Cooking Time: 8 Hours

Servings: ½ Cup

Ingredients:
- ½ beet, peeled and cut into 1/8-inch slices

Directions:
1. Arrange the beet slices flat in a single layer in the Cook & Crisp Basket. Place in the pot and close the Crisping Lid.
2. Press Dehydrate, set the temperature to 135°F and set the time to 8 hours. Select Start/Stop to begin.
3. When dehydrating is complete, remove the basket from the pot and transfer the beet chips to an airtight container.

Nutrition Calories: 35; Total fat: 0g; Saturated fat: 0g; Cholesterol: 0mg; Sodium: 64mg; Carbohydrates: 8g; Fiber: 2g; Protein: 1g

Maple Candied Bacon

Preparation Time: 5 minutes

Cooking Time: 40 Minutes

Servings: 12

Ingredients:
- ½ cup maple syrup
- ¼ cup brown sugar
- Nonstick cooking spray
- 1 pound (12 slices) thick-cut bacon

Directions:

1. Place the Reversible Rack in the pot. Close the Crisping Lid. Preheat the unit by selecting Air Crisp, setting the temperature to 400°F, and setting the time to 5 minutes.
2. Meanwhile, in a small mixing bowl, mix the maple syrup and brown sugar.
3. Once it has preheated, carefully line the Reversible Rack with aluminum foil. Spray the foil with cooking spray.
4. Arrange 4 to 6 slices of bacon on the rack in a single layer. Brush them with the maple syrup mixture.
5. Close the Crisping Lid. Select Air Crisp and set the temperature to 400°F. Set the time to 10 minutes, then select Start/Stop to begin.
6. After 10 minutes, flip the bacon and brush with more maple syrup mixture. Close the Crisping Lid, select Air Crisp, set the temperature to 400°F, and set the time to 10 minutes. Select Start/Stop to begin.
7. Cooking is complete when your desired crispiness is reached. Remove the bacon from the Reversible Rack and transfer to a cooling rack for 10 minutes. Repeat steps 4 through 6 with the remaining bacon.

Nutrition (2 slices) Calories: 451; Total fat: 34g; Saturated fat: 11g; Cholesterol: 51mg; Sodium: 634mg; Carbohydrates: 27g; Fiber: 0g; Protein: 9g

Chili-Ranch Chicken Wings

Preparation Time: 10 minutes

Cooking Time: 28 Minutes

Servings: 4

Ingredients:

- ½ cup of water
- ½ cup hot pepper sauce
- 2 tablespoons unsalted butter, melted
- 1½ tablespoons apple cider vinegar
- 2 pounds frozen chicken wings
- ½ (1-ounce) envelope ranch salad dressing mix
- ½ teaspoon paprika
- Nonstick cooking spray

Directions:

1. Pour the water, hot pepper sauce, butter, and vinegar into the pot. Place the wings in the Cook & Crisp Basket and place the basket in the pot. Assemble the Pressure Lid, making sure the pressure release valve is in the Seal position.
2. Select Pressure and set it to High. Set the time to 5 minutes. Select Start/Stop to begin.
3. When pressure cooking is complete, quick release the pressure by turning the pressure release valve to the

Vent position. Carefully remove the lid when the unit has finished releasing pressure.

4. Sprinkle the chicken wings with the dressing mix and paprika. Coat with cooking spray.

5. Close the Crisping Lid. Select Air Crisp, set the temperature to 375°F and set the time to 15 minutes. Select Start/Stop to begin.

6. After 7 minutes, open the Crisping Lid, then lift the basket and shake the wings. Coat with cooking spray. Lower the basket back into the pot and close the lid to resume cooking until the wings reach your desired crispiness.

Nutrition Calories: 405; Total fat: 30g; Saturated fat: 10g; Cholesterol: 131mg; Sodium: 1782mg; Carbohydrates: 4g; Fiber: 0g; Protein: 28g

Crispy Cheesy Arancini

Preparation Time: 15 minutes

Cooking Time: 45 Minutes

Servings: 6

Ingredients:

- ½ cup extra-virgin olive oil, plus 1 tablespoon
- 1 small yellow onion, diced
- 2 garlic cloves, minced

- 5 cups chicken broth
- ½ cup white wine
- 2 cups arborio rice
- 1½ cups grated Parmesan cheese, plus more for garnish
- 1 cup frozen peas
- 1 teaspoon sea salt
- 1 teaspoon freshly ground black pepper
- 2 cups fresh breadcrumbs
- 2 large eggs

Directions:

1. Select Sear/Sauté and set it to Medium-High. Select Start/Stop to begin. Allow the pot to preheat for 5 minutes.
2. Add 1 tablespoon of oil and the onion to the preheated pot. Cook until soft and translucent, stirring occasionally. Add the garlic and cook for 1 minute.
3. Add the broth, wine, and rice to the pot; stir to incorporate. Assemble the Pressure Lid, making sure the pressure release valve is in the Seal position.
4. Select Pressure and set it to High. Set the time to 7 minutes. Press Start/Stop to begin.
5. When pressure cooking is complete, allow pressure to naturally release for 10 minutes, then quickly release any remaining pressure by turning the pressure release valve

to the Vent position. Carefully remove the lid when the unit has finished releasing pressure.

6. Add the Parmesan cheese, frozen peas, salt, and pepper. Stir vigorously until the rice begins to thicken. Transfer the risotto to a large mixing bowl and let cool.

7. Meanwhile, clean the pot. In a medium mixing bowl, stir together the bread crumbs and the remaining ½ cup of olive oil. In a separate mixing bowl, lightly beat the eggs.

8. Divide the risotto into 12 equal portions and form each one into a ball. Dip each risotto ball in the beaten eggs, then coat in the bread crumb mixture.

9. Arrange half of the arancini in the Cook & Crisp™ Basket in a single layer.

10. Close the Crisping Lid. Select Air Crisp, set the temperature to 400°F and set the time to 10 minutes. Select Start/Stop to begin.

11. Repeat steps 9 and 10 to cook the remaining arancini.

Nutrition Calories: 769; Total fat: 32g; Saturated fat: 9g; Cholesterol: 98mg; Sodium: 1348mg; Carbohydrates: 91g; Fiber: 5g; Protein: 27g

Buffalo Chicken Meatballs

Preparation Time: 10 minutes

Cooking Time: 40 Minutes

Servings: 6

Ingredients:

- 1-pound ground chicken
- 1 carrot, minced
- 2 celery stalks, minced
- ¼ cup crumbled blue cheese
- ¼ cup buffalo sauce
- ¼ cup bread crumbs
- 1 egg
- 2 tablespoons extra-virgin olive oil
- ½ cup of water

Directions:

1. Select Sear/Sauté and set it to High. Select Start/Stop to begin. Allow the pot to preheat for 5 minutes.
2. Meanwhile, in a large mixing bowl, mix the chicken, carrot, celery, blue cheese, buffalo sauce, bread crumbs, and egg. Shape the mixture into 1½-inch meatballs.
3. Pour the olive oil into the preheated pot. Working in batches, place the meatballs in the pot and sear on all

sides until browned. When each batch finishes cooking, transfer to a plate.

4. Place the Cook & Crisp Basket in the pot. Add the water, then place all the meatballs in the basket.

5. Assemble the Pressure Lid, making sure the pressure release valve is in the Seal position. Select Pressure and set to High. Set the time to 5 minutes. Select Start/Stop to begin.

6. When pressure cooking is complete, quick release the pressure by turning the pressure release valve to the Vent position. Carefully remove the lid when the unit has finished releasing pressure.

7. Close the Crisping Lid. Select Air Crisp, set the temperature to 360°F and set the time to 10 minutes. Select Start/Stop to begin.

8. After 5 minutes, open the lid, then lift the basket and shake the meatballs. Lower the basket back into the pot and close the lid to resume cooking until the meatballs achieve your desired crispiness.

Nutrition Calories: 204; Total fat: 13g; Saturated fat: 4g; Cholesterol: 104mg; Sodium: 566mg; Carbohydrates: 5g; Fiber: 1g; Protein: 16g

Loaded Smashed Potatoes

Preparation Time: 10 minutes

Cooking Time: 30 Minutes

Servings: 4

Ingredients:

- 12 ounces baby Yukon Gold potatoes
- 1 teaspoon extra-virgin olive oil
- ¼ cup sour cream
- ¼ cup shredded Cheddar cheese
- 2 slices bacon, cooked and crumbled
- 1 tablespoon chopped fresh chives
- Sea salt

Directions:

1. Place the Cook & Crisp Basket in the pot. Close the Crisping Lid. Preheat the unit by selecting Air Crisp, setting the temperature to 350°F, and setting the time to 5 minutes. Press Start/Stop to begin.
2. Meanwhile, toss the potatoes with the oil until evenly coated.
3. Once the pot and basket are preheated, open the lid, and add the potatoes to the basket. Close the lid, select Air Crisp, set the temperature to 350°F and set the time to 30 minutes. Press Start/Stop to begin.

4. After 15 minutes, open the lid, then lift the basket and shake the potatoes. Lower the basket back into the pot and close the lid to resume cooking.

5. After 15 minutes, check the potatoes for your desired crispiness. They should be fork-tender.

6. Remove the potatoes from the basket. Use a large spoon to lightly crush the potatoes to split them. Top with sour cream, cheese, bacon, and chives, and season with salt.

Nutrition Calories: 154; Total fat: 8g; Saturated fat: 4g; Cholesterol: 19mg; Sodium: 152mg; Carbohydrates: 16g; Fiber: 1g; Protein: 5g

Fried Pickles

Preparation Time: 10 minutes
Cooking Time: 10 Minutes
Servings: 4

Ingredients:
- 20 dill pickle slices
- ¼ cup all-purpose flour

- 1/8 teaspoon baking powder
- 3 tablespoons beer or seltzer water
- 1/8 teaspoon sea salt
- 2 tablespoons water, plus more if needed
- 2 tablespoons cornstarch
- 1½ cups panko breadcrumbs
- 1 teaspoon paprika
- 1 teaspoon garlic powder
- ¼ teaspoon cayenne pepper
- 2 tablespoons canola oil, divided

Directions:

1. Pat the pickle slices dry and place them on a dry plate in the freezer.
2. In a medium bowl, stir together the flour, baking powder, beer, salt, and water. The batter should be the consistency of cake batter. If it is too thick, add more water, 1 teaspoon at a time.
3. Place the cornstarch in a small shallow bowl.
4. In a separate large shallow bowl, combine the breadcrumbs, paprika, garlic powder, and cayenne pepper.
5. Remove the pickles from the freezer. Dredge each one in cornstarch. Tap off any excess, then coat in the batter. Lastly, coat evenly with the bread crumb mixture.

6. Insert the Crisper Basket and close the hood. Select AIR CRISP, set the temperature to 360°F, and set the time to 10 minutes. Select START/STOP to begin preheating.

7. When the unit beeps to signify it has preheated, place the breaded pickles in the basket, stacking them if necessary, and gently brush them with 1 tablespoon of oil. Close the hood and cook for 5 minutes

8. After 5 minutes, shake the basket and gently brush the pickles with the remaining 1 tablespoon of oil. Place the basket back in the unit and close the hood to resume cooking.

9. When cooking is complete, serve immediately.

Nutrition: Calories: 296; Total fat: 10g; Saturated fat: 1g; Cholesterol: 0mg; Sodium: 768mg; Carbohydrates: 44g; Fiber: 3g; Protein: 7g

Meat Recipes

Chicken Alfredo Apples

Preparation Time: 5-10 Minutes

Cooking Time: 20 Minutes

Servings: 4

Ingredients:
- 1 large apple, wedged
- 1 tablespoon lemon juice
- 4 chicken breasts, halved
- 4 teaspoons chicken seasoning
- 4 slices provolone cheese
- 1/4 cup blue cheese, crumbled
- 1/2 cup Alfredo sauce

Directions:

1. Season the chicken in a bowl with chicken seasoning. In another bowl, toss the apple with lemon juice.
2. Take Ninja Grill, arrange it over your kitchen platform, and open the top lid.
3. Arrange the grill grate and close the top lid.
4. Press "GRILL" and select the "MED" grill function. Adjust the timer to 16 minutes and then press "START /STOP." The Ninja will start pre-heating.
5. Ninja is preheated and ready to cook when it starts to beep. After you hear a beep, open the top lid.
6. Arrange the chicken over the grill grate.
7. Close the top lid and cook for 8 minutes. Now open the top lid, flip the chicken.
8. Close the top lid and cook for 8 more minutes.
9. Then, grill the apple in the same manner for 2 minutes per side.
10. Serve the chicken with the apple, blue cheese, and Alfredo sauce.

Nutrition: Calories: 247 Fat: 19g Saturated Fat: 3g Trans Fat: 0g Carbohydrates: 29.5g Fiber: 2g Sodium: 853mg Protein: 14.5g

Baked Soy Chicken

Preparation Time: 5-10 Minutes

Cooking Time: 25 Minutes

Servings: 5-6

Ingredients:

- 1/2 cup soy sauce
- 1/4 cup apple cider vinegar
- 1 clove garlic, minced
- 1 tablespoon cornstarch
- 1 tablespoon cold water
- 1/2 cup white sugar
- 1/4 teaspoon ground black pepper
- 1/2 teaspoon ground ginger
- 12 skinless chicken thighs

Directions:

1. In a mixing bowl, add the cornstarch, water, white sugar, soy sauce, apple cider vinegar, garlic, ginger, and black pepper. Combine the ingredients to mix well with each other.
2. Season the chicken with salt and ground black pepper.

3. Take a multi-purpose pan and lightly grease it with some cooking oil. In the pan, add the chicken and add the soy mixture on top.

4. Take Ninja Foodi Grill, arrange it over your kitchen platform, and open the top lid.

5. Press "BAKE" and adjust the temperature to 350°F. Adjust the timer to 25 minutes and then press "START /STOP." Ninja Foodi will start preheating.

6. Ninja Foodi is preheated and ready to cook when it starts to beep. After you hear a beep, open the top lid.

7. Arrange the pan directly inside the pot.

8. Close the top lid and allow it to cook until the timer reads zero.

9. Serve warm.

Nutrition: Calories: 573 Fat: 19g Saturated Fat: 5g Trans Fat: 0g Carbohydrates: 23.5g Fiber: 1g Sodium: 624mg Protein: 48.5g

Salsa Coconut Chicken

Preparation Time: 5-10 Minutes

Cooking Time: 12 Minutes

Servings: 4

Ingredients:

- ½ cup of coconut milk
- ¼ cup chicken broth
- Black pepper (ground) and salt to taste
- 1 large yellow onion, chopped
- 1 cup salsa Verde
- 4 chicken breasts, cut into 1-inch cubes

Directions:

1. Take Ninja Foodi multi-cooker, arrange it over a cooking platform, and open the top lid.
2. In the pot, add all the ingredients and combine well.
3. Seal the multi-cooker by locking it with the pressure lid; ensure to keep the pressure release valve locked /sealed.
4. Select the "PRESSURE" mode and select the "HI" pressure level. Then, set the timer to 12 minutes and press "STOP /START"; it will start the cooking process by building up inside pressure.
5. When the timer goes off, naturally release inside pressure for about 8-10 minutes. Then, quick-release pressure by adjusting the pressure valve to the VENT.
6. Serve warm and enjoy!

Nutrition: Calories: 548 Fat: 29g Saturated Fat: 5g Trans Fat: 0g Carbohydrates: 7g Fiber: 2.5g Sodium: 847mg Protein: 61g

Chicken Coconut Curry

Preparation Time: 5-10 Minutes

Cooking Time: 12 Minutes

Servings: 4

Ingredients:

- 1 yellow bell pepper, deseeded and thinly sliced
- 1 red bell pepper, deseeded and thinly sliced
- 4 chicken thighs
- Black pepper (ground) and salt to taste
- 1 tablespoon olive oil
- 1 garlic clove, minced
- 1 ½ cups cauliflower rice
- 2 tablespoons red curry paste
- 1 teaspoon ginger paste
- ¼ cup coconut of milk
- ½ cup chicken broth
- 2 tablespoons chopped cilantro to garnish
- 1 lime, cut into wedges to garnish

Directions:

1. Season, the chicken with salt and black pepper.
2. Take Ninja Foodi multi-cooker, arrange it over a cooking platform, and open the top lid.

3. In the pot, add the oil; Select "SEAR /SAUTÉ" mode and select "MD: HI" pressure level. Press "STOP /START." After about 4-5 minutes, the oil will start simmering.

4. Add the meat and stir cook for about 5-6 minutes to brown evenly. Set aside the chicken.

5. Add the bell peppers and cook (while stirring) until it becomes softened. Add the curry paste, ginger, and garlic; stir-cook until fragrant, 1 minute.

6. Add the cauliflower rice, chicken broth, coconut milk; stir the mixture. Add the chicken and combine well.

7. Seal the multi-cooker by locking it with the pressure lid; ensure to keep the pressure release valve locked /sealed.

8. Select "PRESSURE" mode and select the "HI" pressure level. Then, set the timer to 4 minutes and press "STOP /START"; it will start the cooking process by building up inside pressure.

9. When the timer goes off, quick release pressure by adjusting the pressure valve to the VENT. After pressure gets released, open the pressure lid. Serve warm with the cilantro, lime wedges.

Nutrition: Calories: 523 Fat: 28.5g Saturated Fat: 5g Trans Fat: 0g Carbohydrates: 11g Fiber: 2g Sodium: 942mg Protein: 37.5g

Chicken Paillards with Fresh Tomato Sauce

Preparation Time: 5 minutes

Cooking Time: 4 minutes

Serving: 4

Ingredients:

- 2 whole skinless, boneless chicken breasts (each 12 to 16 ounces, or 4 half breasts (each half 6 to 8 ounces
- 1 clove garlic, minced
- 3 fresh basil leaves, minced, plus 4 basil sprigs for garnish
- Coarse salt (kosher or sea and freshly ground black pepper
- 2 tablespoons extra-virgin olive oil

TOMATO SAUCE

- 1 clove garlic, minced
- ½ teaspoon salt, or more to taste
- 1 large ripe red tomato (6 to 8 ounces, seeded (see Tips and cut into ¼-inch dice
- 12 niçoise olives, or 6 black olives, pitted and cut into ¼-inch dice
- 8 fresh basil leaves, thinly slivered
- ¼ cup extra-virgin olive oil

- 1 tablespoon red wine vinegar, or more to taste
- Freshly ground black pepper

Directions:

1. If using whole chicken breasts, divide them in half. Trim any sinews or excess fat off the chicken breasts and discard. Remove the tenders from the breasts and set them aside. Rinse the breasts under cold running water, then drain. Place a breast half between 2 pieces of plastic wrap and gently pound it to a thickness of between ¼ and 1 /8 inch using a meat pounder, the side of a heavy cleaver, a rolling pin, or the bottom of a heavy saucepan. Repeat with the remaining breast halves.

2. Place the garlic and minced basil, ½ teaspoon of salt, and ½ teaspoon of pepper in a bowl and mash to a paste with the back of a spoon. Stir in the olive oil. Brush each paillard on both sides with the garlic and basil mixture and season lightly with salt and pepper.

3. Insert the Grill Grate and close the hood. Select GRILL, set the temperature to HIGH, and set the time to 4 minutes. Select START /STOP to begin preheating.

Nutrition: Calories 299 Fat 20 g Protein 52 g

Korean Chili Pork

Preparation Time: 5-10 minutes
Cooking Time: 8 minutes
Servings: 4

Ingredients:
- 2 pounds pork, cut into 1/8-inch slices
- 5 minced garlic cloves
- 3 tablespoons minced green onion
- 1 yellow onion, sliced
- ½ cup soy sauce
- ½ cup brown sugar
- 3 tablespoons Korean red chili paste or regular chili paste
- 2 tablespoons sesame seeds
- 3 teaspoons black pepper

- Red pepper flakes to taste

Directions:

1. Take a zip-lock bag, add all the ingredients. Shake well and refrigerate for 6-8 hours to marinate.
2. Take Ninja Foodi Grill, orchestrate it over your kitchen stage, and open the top.
3. Mastermind the barbecue mesh and close the top cover.
4. Click Grill and choose the Med grill function. flame broil work. Modify the clock to 8 minutes and press Start /Stop. Ninja Foodi will begin to warm up.
5. Ninja Foodi is preheated and prepared to cook when it begins to signal. After you hear a signal, open the top.
6. Fix finely sliced pork on the barbeque mesh.
7. Cover and cook for 4 minutes. Then open the cover, switch the side of the pork.
8. Cover it and cook for another 4 minutes.
9. Serve warm with chopped lettuce (optional).

Nutrition: Calories: 621, Fat: 31 g, Saturated Fat: 12.5 g, Trans Fat: 0 g, Carbohydrates: 29 g, Fiber: 3 g, Sodium: 1428 mg, Protein: 53 g

Korean Pork

Preparation Time: 5-10 Minutes

Cooking Time: 8 Minutes

Servings: 4

Ingredients:

- 2 pounds pork, cut into 1/8-inch slices
- 5 minced garlic cloves
- 3 tablespoons minced green onion
- 1 yellow onion, sliced
- ½ cup soy sauce
- ½ cup brown sugar
- 3 tablespoons Korean red chili paste or regular chili paste
- 2 tablespoons sesame seeds
- 3 teaspoons black pepper
- Red pepper flakes to taste

Directions:

1. Take a zip-lock bag, add all the ingredients. Shake well and refrigerate for 6-8 hours to marinate.
2. Take Ninja Foodi Grill, arrange it over your kitchen platform, and open the top lid.
3. Arrange the grill grate and close the top lid.

4. Press "GRILL" and select the "MED" grill function. Adjust the timer to 8 minutes and then press "START /STOP." Ninja Foodi will start preheating.

5. Ninja Foodi is preheated and ready to cook when it starts to beep. After you hear a beep, open the top lid.

6. Arrange the sliced pork over the grill grate.

7. Close the top lid and cook for 4 minutes. Now open the top lid, flip the pork.

8. Close the top lid and cook for 4 more minutes.

9. Serve warm with chopped lettuce, optional.

Nutrition: Calories: 621, Fat: 31g, Saturated Fat: 12.5g, Trans Fat: 0g, Carbohydrates: 29g Fiber: 3g, Sodium: 1428mg, Protein: 53g

Garlic Butter Pork

Preparation Time: 10 minutes

Cooking Time: 20 minutes

Servings: 4

Ingredients:
- 1 tablespoon coconut butter
- 1 tablespoon coconut oil

- 2 teaspoons cloves garlic, grated
- 2 teaspoons parsley
- Salt and pepper to taste
- 4 pork chops, sliced into strips

Directions:

1. Combine all the ingredients except the pork strips. Mix well.
2. Marinate the pork in the mixture for 1 hour. Put the pork on the Ninja Foodi basket.
3. Set it inside the pot. Seal with the crisping lid. Choose Air Crisp.
4. Cook at 400°F for 10 minutes.
5. Serving Suggestion:
6. Serve with a fresh garden salad.

Nutrition: Calories: 388, Total Fat: 23.3 g, Saturated Fat: 10.4 g, Cholesterol: 69 mg, Sodium: 57 mg, Total Carbohydrate: 0.5 g, Dietary Fiber: 0.1 g, Total Sugars: 0 g, Protein: 18.1 g, Potassium: 285 mg

Bourbon Barbecue–Glazed Pork Chops

Preparation Time: 5 Minutes

Cooking Time: 35 Minutes

Servings: 4

Ingredients:

- 2 cups ketchup
- ¾ cup bourbon
- ¼ cup apple cider vinegar
- ¼ cup soy sauce
- 1 cup packed brown sugar
- 3 tablespoons Worcestershire sauce
- ½ tablespoon dry mustard powder
- 4 boneless pork chops
- Sea salt
- Freshly ground black pepper

Directions:

1. In a medium saucepan over high heat, combine the ketchup, bourbon, vinegar, soy sauce, sugar, Worcestershire sauce, and mustard powder. Stir to combine and bring to a boil.

2. Reduce the heat to low and simmer, uncovered and stirring occasionally, for 20 minutes. The barbecue sauce will thicken while cooking. Once thickened, remove the pan from the heat and set it aside.

3. While the barbecue sauce is cooking, insert the Grill Grate into the unit and close the hood. Select GRILL, set the temperature to MEDIUM, and set the time to 15 minutes. Select START /STOP to begin preheating.

4. When the unit beeps to signify it has preheated, place the pork chops on the Grill Grate. Close the hood, and cook for 8 minutes. After 8 minutes, flip the pork chops and baste the cooked side with the barbecue sauce. Close the hood, and cook for 5 minutes more.

5. Open the hood, and flip the pork chops again, basting both sides with the barbecue sauce. Close the hood, and cook for the final 2 minutes.

Nutrition: Calories: 361; Total fat: 14g; Saturated fat: 5g; Cholesterol: 55mg; Sodium: 1412mg; Carbohydrates: 26g; Fiber: 0g; Protein: 26g

Roast Beef with Garlic

Preparation Time: 15 minutes

Cooking Time: 1 hour and 20 minutes

Servings: 4

Ingredients:
- 2 lb. beef roast, sliced
- 2 tablespoons vegetable oil
- Salt and pepper to taste
- 6 cloves garlic

Directions:
1. Coat beef roast with oil.

2. Season with salt and pepper.

3. Place them inside the Ninja Foodi Grill pot.

4. Sprinkle garlic on top.

5. Choose the Bake setting.

6. Set it to 400°F and cook for 30 minutes.

7. Reduce the temperature to 375°F and cook for another 40 minutes.

Serving Suggestions: Serve with mashed potato and gravy.

Preparation /Cooking Tips: If refrigerated, let beef come to room temperature 2 hours before cooking.

Nutrition Calories: 390, Fat: 29 g, Carbohydrates: 5 g, Protein: 20 g

Grilled Steak & Potatoes

Preparation Time: 20 minutes

Cooking Time: 50 minutes

Servings: 4

Ingredients:

- 4 potatoes
- 3 sirloin steaks
- ¼ cup avocado oil
- 2 tablespoons steak seasoning
- Salt to taste

Directions:

1. Poke potatoes with a fork.
2. Coat potatoes with half of the avocado oil.
3. Season with salt.
4. Add to the air fryer basket.
5. Choose the air fry function in your Ninja Foodi Grill.
6. Seal the hood and cook at 400°F for 35 minutes.
7. Flip and cook for another 10 minutes.
8. Transfer to a plate.
9. Add the grill grate to the Ninja Foodi Grill.
10. Add steaks to the grill grate.
11. Set it to High.
12. Cook for 7 minutes per side.
13. Serve steaks with potatoes.

Serving Suggestions: Serve with steak sauce and hot sauce.

Preparation /Cooking Tips: Press steaks onto the grill to give it grill marks.

Nutrition: Calories: 245, Fat: 26 g, Carbohydrates: 7 g, Protein: 19 g

Authentic Korean Flank Steak

Preparation Time: 10 minutes

Cooking Time: 10minutes

Servings: 4

Ingredients:
- 1 teaspoon red pepper flakes
- ½ cup and 1 tablespoon soy sauce
- 1½ pounds flank steak
- ¼ cup and 2 tablespoons vegetable oil
- ½ cup of rice wine vinegar
- 3 tablespoons sriracha
- 2 cucumbers, seeded and sliced
- 4 garlic cloves, minced

- 2 tablespoons ginger, minced
- 2 tablespoons honey
- 3 tablespoons sesame oil
- 1 teaspoon sugar
- Salt to taste

Directions:

1. Take a bowl and add ½ cup soy sauce, half of the rice wine, honey, ginger, garlic, 2 tablespoons sriracha, 2 tablespoons sesame oil, and vegetable oil.
2. Mix well, pour half of the mixture over the steak, and rub well.
3. Cover steak and let it sit for 10 minutes.
4. Prepare the salad mix by add remaining rice wine vinegar, sesame oil, sugar red pepper flakes, sriracha sauce, soy sauce, and salt in a salad bowl.
5. Preheat your Ninja Foodi Grill on High, with the timer set to 12 minutes.
6. Transfer steak to your Grill and cook for 6 minutes per side.
7. Slice and serve with the salad mix.
8. Enjoy!

Nutrition: Calories: 327, Fat: 4 g, Saturated Fat: 0.5 g, Carbohydrates: 33 g, Fiber: 1 g, Sodium: 142 mg, Protein: 24 g

Grilled Beef Burgers

Preparation Time: 5-10 Minutes

Cooking Time: 10 Minutes

Servings: 4

Ingredients:

- 4 ounces cream cheese
- 4 slices bacon, cooked and crumbled
- 2 seeded jalapeño peppers, stemmed, and minced
- ½ cup shredded Cheddar cheese
- ½ teaspoon chili powder
- ¼ teaspoon paprika
- ¼ teaspoon ground black pepper
- 2 pounds ground beef
- 4 hamburger buns
- 4 slices pepper Jack cheese
- Optional - Lettuce, sliced tomato, and sliced red onion

Directions:

1. In a mixing bowl, combine the peppers, Cheddar cheese, cream cheese, and bacon until well combined.
2. Prepare the ground beef into 8 patties. Add the cheese mixture onto four of the patties; arrange a second patty on top of each to prepare four burgers. Press gently.

3. In another bowl, combine the chili powder, paprika, and pepper. Sprinkle the mixture onto the sides of the burgers.

4. Take Ninja Foodi Grill, arrange it over your kitchen platform, and open the top lid.

5. Arrange the grill grate and close the top lid.

6. Press "GRILL" and select the "HIGH" grill function. Adjust the timer to 4 minutes and then press "START /STOP." Ninja Foodi will start pre-heating.

7. Ninja Foodi is preheated and ready to cook when it starts to beep. After you hear a beep, open the top lid.

8. Arrange the burgers over the grill grate.

9. Close the top lid and allow it to cook until the timer reads zero. Cook for 3-4 more minutes, if needed.

10. Cook until the food thermometer reaches 145°F. Serve warm.

11. Serve warm with buns. Add your choice of toppings: pepper Jack cheese, lettuce, tomato, and red onion.

Nutrition: Calories: 783, Fat: 38g, Saturated Fat: 16g, Trans Fat: 0g, Carbohydrates: 25g, Fiber: 3g, Sodium: 1259mg, Protein: 57.5g

Middle Eastern Lamb Stew

Preparation Time: 10 minutes

Cooking Time: 20 minutes

Servings: 4

Ingredients:
- 2 tablespoons olive oil
- 1½ lb. lamb stew meat, sliced into cubes
- 1 onion, diced
- 6 garlic cloves, chopped
- 1 teaspoon cumin
- 1 teaspoon coriander
- 1 teaspoon turmeric
- 1 teaspoon cinnamon

- Salt and pepper to taste
- 2 tablespoons tomato paste
- ¼ cup red wine vinegar
- 2 tablespoons honey
- 1¼ cups chicken broth
- 15 oz. chickpeas, rinsed and drained
- ¼ cup raisins

Directions:

1. Choose Sauté on the Ninja Foodi. Add the oil. Cook the onion for 3 minutes.
2. Add the lamb and seasonings. Cook for 5 minutes, stirring frequently.
3. Stir in the rest of the ingredients. Cover the pot. Set it to Pressure.
4. Cook on high pressure for 50 minutes. Release the pressure naturally.

Nutrition: Calories: 867, Total Fat: 26.6 g, Saturated Fat: 6.3 g, Cholesterol: 153 mg, Sodium: 406 mg, Total Carbohydrate: 87.4 g, Dietary Fiber: 20.4 g, Total Sugars: 27.9 g, Protein: 71.2 g, Potassium: 1815 mg

Chorizo Cashew Soup

Preparation Time: 30-35 Minutes

Cooking Time: 70 Minutes

Servings: 5-6

Ingredients:

- 2 shallots, sliced
- 3 cloves garlic, minced
- 3 chorizo sausage, chopped
- 28 ounces fire-roasted diced tomatoes
- ½ cup ripe tomatoes
- tablespoon red wine vinegar
- ½ cup thinly sliced fresh basil
- 4 cups beef broth
- ½ cup raw cashews
- tablespoon olive oil
- teaspoon salt
- ½ teaspoon ground black pepper

Directions:

1. Take your Ninja Foodi and place it over a dry kitchen platform. Plug it in and open the lid.
2. Pour the oil into the pot. Press "SEAR /SAUTÉ" cooking function. Adjust temperature level to "MD: HI".

3. Press the "START /STOP" button to start the cooking process. It will take 3-5 minutes to pre-heat.
4. When the oil is simmering, add the chorizo; stir and cook until crisp. Remove and transfer to a plate lined with a paper towel.
5. Add the garlic and onions; stir and cook to soften and turn translucent for 4-5 minutes. Season with salt.
6. Stir in the wine vinegar, broth, diced tomatoes, cashews, tomatoes, and black pepper.
7. Close the top by placing the pressing lid. Do not forget to set the pressure valve to a locked position.
8. Press the "PRESSURE" cooking function. Adjust the temperature level to "HI".
9. Adjust cooking time to 8 minutes. Press the "START /STOP" button to start the cooking process.
10. After cooking time is over, set the pressure valve to VENT position to release the build-up pressure quicker.
11. Add the mixture to a blender; blend to make a smooth soup.
12. Divide into serving plates or bowls; serve warm top with some basil and crisped chorizo.

Nutrition: Calories 347, Fat 22g, Carbohydrates 17g, Fiber 4g, Protein 14g

Bacon Potato Salad

Preparation Time: 20Minutes

Cooking Time: 70 Minutes

Servings: 5-6

Ingredients:

- 6 slices smoked bacon, chopped
- 2 red onions, sliced
- 6 red potatoes, peeled and quartered
- ½ cup of water
- teaspoon flat-leaf parsley, chopped
- teaspoons mustard
- ½ cup apple cider vinegar
- tablespoons honey
- teaspoon salt
- 3 teaspoon black pepper

Directions:

1. Take your Ninja Foodi and place it over a dry kitchen platform. Plug it in and open the lid.
2. Press "SEAR /SAUTÉ" cooking function. Adjust temperature level to "MD: HI".
3. Press the "START /STOP" button to start the cooking process. It will take 3-5 minutes to pre-heat.

4. In the pot, add the bacon and cook until crispy on both sides for 3-4 minutes. Set aside.

5. In a mixing bowl (medium-large size), combine honey, salt, mustard, vinegar, water, and black pepper.

6. In the pot, combine the potatoes, chopped bacon, honey mixture, and onions; stir the mixture.

7. Close the top by placing the pressing lid. Do not forget to set the temperature valve in a locked or sealed position.

8. Press the "PRESSURE" cooking function. Adjust and set pressure level to "HI".

9. Adjust cooking time to 6 minutes. Press the "START /STOP" button to start the cooking process.

10. After cooking time is over, allow the build-up pressure to get released for around 10 minutes in a natural manner. Then, set the pressure valve to VENT position in order to release the remaining pressure quicker.

11. Divide into serving plates or bowls; serve warm with some parsley on top.

Nutrition: Calories 413, Fat 17g, Carbohydrates 47g, Fiber 4g, Protein 13g

Fish and Seafood Recipes

Cedar-Plank Salmon

Preparation Time: 30 Minutes

Cooking Time: 2 Hours and 30 Minutes

Servings: 6

Ingredients:
- 2 Tbsp grainy mustard
- 2 Tbsp mild honey or pure maple syrup
- 1 teaspoon Minced rosemary
- 1 Tbsp grated lemon zest
- 1 (2-pounds) salmon fillet with skin (1½ inches thick)

Directions:

1. Splash cedar Ninja oven broiling board in water to cover 2 HRS, keeping it inundated.
2. Plan barbecue for direct-heat cooking over medium-hot charcoal. Open vents on the base and top of a charcoal Ninja oven broil.
3. Mix mustard, nectar, rosemary, pizzazz, and ½ teaspoon every one of salt and pepper. Spread blends on the substance side of salmon and let remain at room temperature 15MIN.
4. Put salmon on board, skin side down. Barbecue, secured with a cover, until salmon is simply cooked through and edges are seared, 13 to 15MIN. Let salmon remain on board 5MIN before serving.

Nutrition: Calories 240, Fat 15g, Carbohydrate 0g, Protein 23g.

Grilled Coconut Shrimp with Shishito Peppers

Preparation Time: 25 Minutes
Cooking Time: 25 Minutes
Servings: 4

Ingredients:

- 6 garlic cloves, finely grated
- 1 Tbsp. finely grated lime zest
- ¼ cup low sodium
- ¼ cup grapeseed or vegetable oil
- 1 lb. large shrimp, peeled, deveined
- ½ cup toasted unsweetened shredded coconut
- 8 - oz. shish to peppers
- ½ cup basil leaves
- ¼ cup fresh lime juice
- Flaky sea salt

Directions:

1. Mix garlic, lime get-up-and-go, soy sauce, and ¼ cup oil in a medium bowl. Add shrimp and hurl to cover. Include ½ cup coconut and hurl again to cover. Let sit while the Ninja oven broil warms, in any event, 5MIN and up to 30MIN.

2. Set up a Ninja oven broil for high warmth, delicately oil grind.

3. Cautiously organize shrimp in an even layer on the mesh. Ninja oven broil, cautiously turning part of the way through, until hazy and daintily singed, about 2MIN. A portion of the coconuts will tumble off all the while, and that is alright. Move to a serving platter.

4. Ninja oven broil peppers, turning every so often and being mindful so as not to let them fall through the mesh until delicately roasted all over about 6MIN. Move to platter with shrimp.

5. Top shrimp and peppers with basil, shower with a lime squeeze, and sprinkle with ocean salt and more coconut.

Nutrition: Calories 82, Fat 7g, Carbohydrate 4g, Protein 2g.

Clams with Spicy Tomato Broth and Garlic Mayo

Preparation Time: 10 Minutes
Cooking Time: 50 Minutes
Servings: 4

Ingredients:

- ½ lemon
- 5 - garlic cloves, 1 whole, 4 thinly sliced
- ½ cup mayonnaise
- Kosher salt

- ¼ cup plus 3 Tbsp. extra-virgin olive oil
- 2 - large shallots, thinly sliced
- red Chile (such as Holland or Fresno), thinly sliced, or½ tsp. crushed red pepper flakes
- Tbsp. tomato paste
- cups cherry tomatoes
- 1 - cup dry white wine
- 36 - littleneck clams, scrubbed
- 6 - Tbsp. unsalted butter, cut into pieces
- Tbsp. finely chopped chives
- thick slices of country-style bread

Directions:

1. Set up a Ninja Foodi oven broil for medium warmth. Finely grind the get-up-and-go from lemon half into a little bowl, at that point crush in the juice. Finely grind the entire garlic clove into a bowl and blend in mayonnaise. Season garlic mayo with salt and put it in a safe spot.

2. Spot a huge cast-iron skillet on the Ninja Foodi oven broil and warmth ¼ cup oil in a skillet. Include cut garlic, shallots, and Chile and cook, mixing regularly, until simply mollified, about 2MIN. Include tomato glue and cook, mixing frequently, until glue obscures

somewhat, around 1 MIN. Include tomatoes and a touch of salt and cook, mixing every so often, until tomatoes mellow and discharge their juices, about 4MIN. Include wine and cook until it is nearly decreased considerably and no longer scents boozy about 3MIN.

3. Add shellfishes and margarine to the skillet and spread. Cook until shellfishes have opened, 6–10MIN, contingent upon the size of mollusks and warmth level. Expel skillet from Ninja Foodi oven broil; dispose of any mollusks that do not open. Sprinkle with chives.

4. In the interim, shower bread with the staying 3 Tbsp. oil and season softly with salt. Barbecue until brilliant earthy colored and fresh, about 3MIN per side.

5. Serve mollusks with toasted bread and saved garlic mayo.

Nutrition: Calories 282, Fat 10g, Carbohydrate 0g, Protein 20g.

Grilled Swordfish with Tomatoes and Oregano

Preparation Time: 10 Minutes
Cooking Time: 40 Minutes
Servings: 4

Ingredients:

- ½ cup plus 2 Tbsp. extra-virgin olive oil, plus more for the grill
- 2 - Tbsp. pine nuts
- 2 - (12-oz.) swordfish steaks, about 1" thick
- Kosher salt, freshly ground pepper
- ¼ cup red wine vinegar
- 2 - Tbsp. drained capers, finely chopped
- - Tbsp. finely chopped oregano, plus 2 sprigs for serving
- ½ tsp. honey
- - large ripe heirloom tomatoes, halved, thickly sliced

Directions:

1. Set up a Ninja Foodi oven broil for medium-high warmth; delicately oil grind. Toast pine nuts in a dry little skillet over medium warmth, shaking frequently, until brilliant, about 4MIN. Let cool and put in a safe spot for serving.

2. Pat swordfish dry and season did with salt and pepper. Spot on a rimmed preparing sheet and let sit at room temperature 15MIN.

3. Then, whisk vinegar, tricks, hacked oregano, nectar, and½ cup oil in a little bowl to consolidate; put the marinade in a safe spot. Mastermind tomatoes on a rimmed platter, covering somewhat; put in a safe spot.

4. Rub swordfish done with the staying 2 Tbsp. oil and Ninja Foodi oven broil, undisturbed, until barbecue marks show up, about 4MIN. cautiously turn over and cook on the second side until fish is misty entirely through, about 4MIN. Move to saved platter with tomatoes and top with oregano branches. Season with increasingly salt and pepper. Pour held marinade over and let sit in any event 15MIN and if 60 minutes. To serve, disperse saved pine nuts over.

Nutrition: Calories 210, Fat 10g, Carbohydrate 0g, Protein 30g.

Grilled Spiced Snapper with Mango and Red Onion Salad

Preparation Time: 10 Minutes

Cooking Time: 30 Minutes

Servings: 4

Ingredients:

- (5-lb.) or 2 (2½-lb.) head-on whole fish, cleaned
- Kosher salt
- 1 /3 - cup chat masala, vadouvan, or tandoori spice
- 1 /3 - cup vegetable oil, plus more for the grill
- 1 - ripe but firm mango, peeled, cut into irregular 1½" pieces
- 1 - small red onion, thinly sliced, rinsed
- 1 - bunch cilantro, coarsely chopped
- - Tbsp. fresh lime juice
- Extra-virgin olive oil
- Lime wedges (for serving)

Directions:

1. Spot fish on a cutting board and pat dry altogether with paper towels. With a sharp blade, make slices across on an askew along the body each 2" on the two sides, chopping right down to the bones. Season fish liberally all around with salt. Coat fish with flavor blend, pressing

on more if necessary. Let sit at room temperature 20MIN.

2. In the interim, set up a Ninja Foodi oven broil for medium-high warmth. Clean and oil grind.

3. Shower the two sides of fish with staying 1 /3 cup vegetable oil to cover. Ninja Foodi oven broils fish undisturbed, 10MIN. Lift up somewhat from one edge to check whether the skin is puffed and softly roasted and effectively discharges from the mesh. If not exactly prepared, take off alone for another MIN or somewhere in the vicinity and attempt once more. When it is prepared, delicately slide 2 huge metal spatulas underneath and turn over. Barbecue fish until the opposite side is daintily roasted and skin is puffed, 8– 12MIN, contingent upon the size of the fish. Move to a platter.

4. Sling mango, onion, cilantro, lime juice, and a major spot of salt in a medium bowl. Sprinkle with a touch of olive oil and sling again to cover. Disperse a mango plate of mixed greens over fish and present with lime wedges for pressing over.

Nutrition: Calories 224, Fat 9g, Carbohydrate 17g, Protein 24g.

Grilled Shrimp, Zucchini, and Tomatoes with Feta

Preparation Time: 30 Minutes
Cooking Time: 2 Hours and 30 Minutes
Servings: 6

Ingredients:
- 1 - large garlic clove, finely grated
- 2 - Tsp finely chopped oregano
- ¾ teaspoon kosher salt
- ¼ teaspoon crushed red pepper flakes
- 2 - Tbsp olive oil, plus more for a grill basket
- 10 - jumbo shrimp (about 8 ounces), peeled, deveined, tails left on

- 1 - medium zucchini (about 8 ounces), sliced into ¼" rounds
- 1 - pint cherry tomatoes
- 2 - pita pockets
- 1 /3 - cup crumbled feta (about 1.5 ounces)
- Special Equipment
- A flat grill basket (about 13½ x 8½")

Directions:

1. Set up a Ninja Foodi oven broil for high warmth. Whisk garlic, oregano, salt, red pepper, and 2 Tbsp. oil in an enormous bowl. Include shrimp, zucchini, and tomatoes and hurl to cover.

2. Brush wires of Ninja Foodi oven broil container with oil, at that point, include shrimp blend. Mastermind in an even layer and close container. Spot barbecue container on Ninja Foodi oven broil and cook, turning regularly until shrimp are completely cooked through and zucchini and tomatoes are delicately singed about 6MIN.

3. In the meantime, barbecue pita just until warm and toasted.

4. Move shrimp blend to an enormous bowl and hurl until covered with tomato juices. Partition among plates and top with feta. Present with pita close by.

Nutrition: Calories 178, Fat 3g, Carbohydrate 12g, Protein 24g.

Vegetarian Recipes

Penne with Mushrooms and Gruyère

Preparation Time: 10 Minutes

Cooking Time: 30 Minutes

Servings: 4

Ingredients:

- 8 ounces penne pasta
- 1 (12–fluid ounce) can evaporate milk, divided
- 1¼ cups water or **Roasted Vegetable Stock**
- 1½ teaspoons kosher salt (or ¾ teaspoon fine salt)
- 1 large egg
- 1½ teaspoons cornstarch
- 8 ounces Gruyère cheese, shredded
- 1 recipe **Sautéed Mushrooms**
- 2 tablespoons chopped fresh parsley
- 3 tablespoons sour cream
- 1½ cups panko breadcrumbs
- 3 tablespoons melted unsalted butter
- 3 tablespoons grated Parmesan or similar cheese

Directions:

1. Pour the penne into the inner pot. Add 6 fluid ounces (¾ cup) of evaporated milk, water, and salt.

2. Lock the Pressure Lid into place, making sure the valve is set to Seal. Select Pressure and adjust the pressure to High and the Cooking Time to 4 minutes. Press Start.

3. While the pasta cooks, in a small bowl, thoroughly whisk the remaining 6 fluid ounces (¾ cup) of evaporated milk with the egg. In another small bowl, sprinkle the cornstarch over the Gruyère cheese and toss to coat.

4. After cooking, let the pressure release naturally for 3 minutes, then quick release any remaining pressure. Carefully unlock and remove the Pressure Lid.

5. Add the milk-egg mixture and a large handful of the Gruyère cheese and stir to melt the cheese. Add the rest of the Gruyère cheese in 3 or 4 batches, stirring to melt after each addition. Stir in the mushrooms, parsley, and sour cream.

6. In a medium bowl, stir together the panko, melted butter, and Parmesan cheese. Sprinkle the panko over the pasta.

7. Close the Crisping Lid. Select Broil and adjust the time to 5 minutes. Press Start. When done, the topping should be brown and crisp; if not, broil for 1 to 2 minutes more. Serve immediately.

Nutrition Calories: 804, Total fat: 39g, Saturated fat: 22g, Cholesterol: 169mg, Sodium: 1437mg, Carbohydrates: 74g, Fiber: 3g, Protein: 38

Easy Eggplant Parmesan

Preparation Time: 15 Minutes

Cooking Time: 40 Minutes

Servings: 4

Ingredients:

- 1 large eggplant, cut into ¾-inch-thick rounds
- 2 teaspoons kosher salt (or 1 teaspoon fine salt)
- 3 tablespoons melted unsalted butter
- 1½ cups panko breadcrumbs
- 1 /3 cup grated Parmesan or similar cheese
- 2 cups **Marinara Sauce**
- 1 cup shredded mozzarella cheese

Directions:

1. Sprinkle the eggplant slices on both sides with the salt and place on a wire rack over a rimmed baking sheet to drain for 5 to 10 minutes.
2. While the eggplant drains, in a medium bowl, stir together the melted butter, panko, and Parmesan cheese. Set aside.
3. Rinse the eggplant slices and blot them dry. Place them in a single layer (as much as possible) in the inner pot and cover them with the marinara sauce.

4. Lock the Pressure Lid into place, making sure the valve is set to Seal. Select Pressure and adjust the pressure to High and the Cooking Time to 5 minutes. Press Start.

5. After cooking, use a quick pressure release. Carefully unlock and remove the Pressure Lid.

6. Cover the eggplant slices with the mozzarella cheese.

7. Close the Crisping Lid. Select Bake /Roast and adjust the temperature to 375°F and the Cooking Time to 2 minutes. Press Start.

8. When cooking is complete, open the lid and sprinkle the eggplant and cheese with the panko mixture. Close the Crisping Lid again. Select Bake /Roast and adjust the temperature to 375°F and the Cooking Time to 8 minutes. Press Start. When done, the topping should be brown and crisp; if not, broil for 1 to 2 minutes more. Serve immediately.

Nutrition: Calories: 434, Total fat: 20g, Saturated fat: 11g, Cholesterol: 52mg, Sodium: 906mg, Carbohydrates: 47g, Fiber: 8g, Protein: 18g

Mediterranean White Bean Salad

Preparation Time: 10 Minutes

Cooking Time: 30 Minutes

Servings: 4

Ingredients:

- 1 tablespoon plus 1 teaspoon kosher salt (or 2 teaspoons fine salt), divided
- 14 ounces dried cannellini beans
- 4 tablespoons plus 1 teaspoon extra-virgin olive oil, divided
- 1-quart water

- 3 tablespoons freshly squeezed lemon juice
- 1 teaspoon ground cumin
- ¼ teaspoon freshly ground black pepper
- 1 medium red or green bell pepper, chopped (about 1 cup)
- 1 large celery stalk, chopped (about ½ cup)
- 3 or 4 scallions, chopped (about 1/3 cup)
- 1 large tomato, seeded and chopped (about ½ cup)
- ½ cucumber, peeled, seeded, and chopped (about ¾ cup)
- 1 cup crumbled feta cheese (optional)
- 2 tablespoons minced fresh mint
- ¼ cup minced fresh parsley

Directions:

1. In a large bowl, dissolve 1 tablespoon of kosher salt (or 1½ teaspoons of fine salt) in 1 quart of water. Add the beans and soak at room temperature for 8 to 24 hours.

2. Drain and rinse the beans. Place them in the inner pot. Add 1 teaspoon of olive oil and stir to coat the beans. Add the 1 quart of water and ½ teaspoon of kosher salt (or ¼ teaspoon of fine salt).

3. Lock the Pressure Lid into place, making sure the valve is set to Seal. Select Pressure and adjust the pressure to High and the Cooking Time to 5 minutes. Press Start.

4. While the beans cook and the pressure releases, in a small jar with a tight-fitting lid, combine the lemon juice and 3 tablespoons of olive oil. Add the cumin, the remaining ½ teaspoon of kosher salt (or ¼ teaspoon of fine salt), and the pepper. Cover the jar and shake the dressing until thoroughly combined. (Alternatively, whisk the dressing in a small bowl, but it is easier to make it in a jar.)

5. After cooking, let the pressure release naturally for 10 minutes, then quickly release any remaining pressure. Carefully unlock and remove the Pressure Lid.

6. Drain the beans and pour them into a bowl. Immediately pour the dressing over the beans and toss to coat. Let cool to room temperature, stirring occasionally.

7. Add the bell pepper, celery, scallions, tomato, cucumber, and feta cheese (if using; omit for a dairy-free and vegan dish) to the beans. Toss gently. Right before serving, add the mint and parsley and toss to combine.

Nutrition: Calories: 489, Total fat: 16g, Saturated fat: 2g, Cholesterol: 0mg, Sodium: 622mg, Carbohydrates: 66g, Fiber: 27g, Protein: 25g

Cajun Twice-Baked Potatoes

Preparation Time: 10 Minutes

Cooking Time: 45 Minutes

Servings: 4

Ingredients:

- 4 small russet potatoes, scrubbed clean
- ¼ cup heavy (whipping) cream
- ¼ cup sour cream
- ½ cup chopped roasted red pepper
- 1 teaspoon **Cajun Seasoning Mix** or a store-bought mix
- 1½ cups shredded white Cheddar cheese
- 4 scallions, white and green parts, chopped, divided
- 1 /3 cup grated Parmesan or similar cheese

Directions:

1. Pour 1 cup of water into the inner pot. Place the Reversible Rack in the pot in the lower position and place the potatoes on top.
2. Lock the Pressure Lid into place, making sure the valve is set to Seal. Select Pressure and adjust the pressure to High and the Cooking Time to 10 minutes. Press Start.

3. After cooking, let the pressure release naturally for 5 minutes, then quickly release any remaining pressure. Carefully unlock and remove the Pressure Lid.

4. Using tongs, transfer the potatoes to a cutting board. When cool enough to handle, slice off a ½-inch strip from the top, the long side of each potato. Scoop the flesh into a large bowl, including the flesh from the tops. Add the heavy cream and sour cream. Using a potato masher, mash until smooth. Stir in the roasted red pepper, seasoning, and Cheddar cheese. Set aside about 2 tablespoons of the green part of the scallions and stir the rest into the potatoes. Spoon the mashed potato mixture into the potato skins, mounding it slightly. Sprinkle the Parmesan evenly over the tops.

5. Empty the water out of the inner pot and return it to the base.

6. Place the Cook & Crisp™ Basket into the pot. Close the Crisping Lid. Select Air Crisp and adjust the temperature to 375°F and the time to 2 minutes to preheat. Press Start.

7. When it is heated, open the lid, and place the potatoes in the basket. Close the Crisping Lid. Select Air Crisp and adjust the temperature to 375°F and the Cooking Time to 15 minutes. Press Start.

8. When done, the potatoes should be lightly browned and crisp on top. Let cool for a few minutes and serve garnished with the reserved scallions.

Nutrition: Calories: 429, Total fat: 25g, Saturated fat: 15g, Cholesterol: 80mg, Sodium: 418mg, Carbohydrates: 35g, Fiber: 3g, Protein: 18g

"Spanish" Rice and Beans

Preparation Time: 5 Minutes

Cooking Time: 30 Minutes

Servings: 4

Ingredients:

- 3 tablespoons olive oil
- 1 small onion, chopped (about 2 /3 cup)
- 2 large garlic cloves, minced
- 1 jalapeño pepper, seeded and chopped (about 2 tablespoons)
- 1 cup long-grain white rice, thoroughly rinse
- 1 /3 cup red salsa
- ¼ cup tomato sauce
- ½ cup Roasted Vegetable Stock, low-sodium vegetable broth, or water
- 1 teaspoon Mexican /Southwestern Seasoning Mix, or store-bought mix
- 1 (16-ounce) can pinto beans, drained and rinsed
- 1 teaspoon kosher salt (or ½ teaspoon fine salt)
- 1 tablespoon chopped fresh cilantro (optional)

Directions:

1. On your Ninja Grill, select Sear /Sauté and adjust to Medium to preheat the inner pot. Press Start. Allow the

pot to preheat for 5 minutes. Pour in the olive oil and heat until shimmering. Add the onion, garlic, and jalapeño. Cook for 2 minutes, stirring occasionally, or until fragrant and beginning to soften. Stir in the rice, salsa, tomato sauce, vegetable stock, seasoning, pinto beans, and salt. (If using water, add another ½ teaspoon of kosher salt or ¼ teaspoon of fine salt).

2. Lock the Pressure Lid into place, making sure the valve is set to Seal. Select Pressure and adjust the pressure to High and the Cooking Time to 6 minutes. Press Start.

3. After cooking, let the pressure release naturally for 10 minutes, then quickly release any remaining pressure. Carefully unlock and remove the Pressure Lid. Stir in the cilantro (if using) and serve.

Nutrition Calories: 384, Total fat: 12g, Saturated fat: 2g, Cholesterol: 0mg, Sodium: 1089mg, Carbohydrates: 60g, Fiber: 7g, Protein: 10g

Dessert Recipes

Blueberry Lemon Muffins

Preparation Time: 5 minutes
Cooking Time: 10 minutes
Serving: 12

Ingredients:
- 1 tsp. vanilla

- Juice and zest of 1 lemon
- 2 eggs
- 1 C. blueberries
- ½ C. cream
- ¼ C. avocado oil
- ½ C. monk fruit
- 2 ½ C. almond flour

Directions:

1. Mix monk fruit and flour.
2. In another bowl, mix vanilla, egg, lemon juice, and cream. Add mixtures together and blend well.
3. Spoon batter into cupcake holders.
4. Air Frying.
5. Place in the air fryer. Bake 10 minutes at 320 degrees, checking at 6 minutes to ensure you do not over bake them.

Nutrition: Calories 317, Fat 11 g, Protein 3 g, Sugar 5 g

Grilled Pound Cake with Berry Compote

Preparation Time: 5 minutes

Cooking Time: 30 minutes

Serving: 4

Ingredients:

FOR THE POUND CAKE

- 1 cup butter, softened
- 1 cup sugar
- 4 eggs
- 1 tsp. vanilla
- pinch of salt
- 2 cups flour

Directions:

1. Mix the compote ingredients in a saucepan. Bring to a boil, stirring well. Remove from the heat and set aside.
2. In a mixing bowl, mix the butter and sugar until fluffy.
3. Add the eggs one at a time, mixing well between each egg.
4. Add the vanilla and salt.
5. Stir in the flour until well combined, but do not over mix.
6. Scoop and level the pound cake batter out onto a sheet pan.
7. Bake until the cake is golden brown.
8. Once the pound cake is cooled, cut into 3-inch squares.

9. Heat the grill to medium and grill the pound cakes lightly. Serve warm with the compote drizzled over the top.

Nutrition: Calories 317, Fat 11 g, Protein 3 g, Sugar 5 g

Sweet Cream Cheese Wontons

Preparation Time: 5 minutes

Cooking Time: 5 minutes

Serving: 16

Ingredients:
- 1 egg mixed with a bit of water
- Wonton wrappers
- ½ C. powdered erythritol
- 8 ounces softened cream cheese
- Olive oil

Directions:
1. Mix sweetener and cream cheese.
2. Layout 4 wontons at a time and cover with a dish towel to prevent drying out.

3. Place ½ of a teaspoon of cream cheese mixture into each wrapper.

4. Dip finger into egg /water mixture and fold diagonally to form a triangle. Seal edges well.

5. Repeat with theremaining ingredients.

6. Insert the Crisper Basket and close the hood. Select AIR CRISP, set the temperature to 400°F, and set the time to 5 minutes. Select START /STOP to begin preheating.

7. Air frying. Place filled wontons into the air fryer and cook 5 minutes at 400 degrees, shaking halfway through cooking.

Nutrition: Calories 303, Fat 3 g, Protein 1 g, Sugar 4 g

Air Fryer Cinnamon Rolls

Preparation Time: 15 minutes

Cooking Time: 5 minutes

Serving: 8

Ingredients:
- 1 ½ tbsp. cinnamon

- ¾ C. brown sugar
- ¼ C. melted coconut oil
- 1-pound frozen bread dough, thawed

Directions:

1. Layout bread dough and roll it out into a rectangle. Brush melted ghee over the dough and leave a 1-inch border along the edges.
2. Mix cinnamon and sweetener and then sprinkle over dough.
3. Roll dough tightly and slice into 8 pieces. Let sit 1-2 hours to rise.
4. To make the glaze, simply mix ingredients till smooth.
5. Air Frying.
6. Once rolls rise, place into the air fryer and cook for 5 minutes at 350 degrees.
7. Serve rolls drizzled in cream cheese glaze. Enjoy

Nutrition: Calories 390, Fat 8 g, Protein 1 g, Sugar 7 g

Smoked Apple Crumble

Preparation Time: 5 minutes

Cooking Time: 45 minutes

Serving: 4

Ingredients:

Filling

- 4–5 large Honeycrisp apples, peeled and sliced
- juice from ½ lemon
- 2 Tbsp. flour
- 1/3 cup sugar
- 1 Tbsp. ground cinnamon
- 1 tsp. ground nutmeg

Directions:

1. Insert the Grill Grate and close the hood. Select GRILL, set temperature to HIGH, and set time to 40 minutes. Select START /STOP to begin preheating.

2. Place apples in a large mixing bowl and toss with lemon juice. Then add in flour, sugar, cinnamon, and nutmeg, and mix thoroughly.

3. Pour apples into a greased cast-iron pan. Set mixture aside.

4. Using the now-empty mixing bowl, combine brown sugar, flour, oatmeal, caramel chips, pecans, cinnamon, baking powder, and salt for the topping.

5. Using a pastry blender or large fork, cut the cold butter into the topping mix.

6. Cover apples with topping mixture.

7. Add one or two pecan wood chunks to the hot coals. Place apple crumble over the Roasting Rack.

8. Close the hood and bake until apples start to bubble, and topping begins to brown (about 45 minutes.

9. Remove from grill and serve warm with French vanilla ice cream.

Nutrition: Calories 317, Fat 11 g, Protein 3 g, Sugar 5 g

Bread Pudding with Cranberry

Preparation Time: 5 minutes

Cooking Time: 35 minutes

Serving: 4

Ingredients:

- 1-1/2 cups milk
- 2-1/2 eggs
- 1/2 cup cranberries1 teaspoon butter
- 1/4 cup and 2 tablespoons white sugar
- 1/4 cup golden raisins
- 1/8 teaspoon ground cinnamon
- 3/4 cup heavy whipping cream
- 3/4 teaspoon lemon zest
- 3/4 teaspoon kosher salt
- 3/4 French baguettes, cut into 2-inch slices
- 3/8 vanilla bean, split and seeds scraped away

Directions:

1. Lightly grease the baking pan of the air fryer with cooking spray. Spread baguette slices, cranberries, and raisins.
2. In a blender, blend well vanilla bean, cinnamon, salt, lemon zest, eggs, sugar, and cream. Pour over baguette slices. Let it soak for an hour.

3. Cover pan with foil.

4. For 35 minutes, cook at 330°F.

5. Let it rest for 10 minutes. Serve and enjoy.

Nutrition: Calories 590, Fat 25 g, Protein 17 g, Sugar 9 g

Black and White Brownies

Preparation Time: 10 minutes

Cooking Time: 20 minutes

Serving: 8

Ingredients:
- 1 egg

- ¼ cup brown sugar
- 2 tablespoons white sugar
- 2 tablespoons safflower oil
- 1 teaspoon vanilla
- ¼ cup of cocoa powder
- 1/3 cup all-purpose flour
- ¼ cup white chocolate chips
- Nonstick baking spray with flour

Directions:

1. In a medium bowl, beat the egg with the brown sugar and white sugar. Beat in the oil and vanilla.
2. Add the cocoa powder and flour and stir just until combined. Fold in the white chocolate chips.
3. Spray a 6-by-6-by-2-inch baking pan with nonstick spray. Spoon the brownie batter into the pan.
4. Bake for 20 minutes or until the brownies are set when lightly touched with a finger. Let cool for 30 minutes before slicing to serve.

Nutrition: Calories 317, Fat 11 g, Protein 3 g, Sugar 5 g

Conclusion

Thanks for making it to the end of this book. Ninja grill cooking is a fun way to eat great food. It's also a great way to get healthier meals, cheaper food, and to get your family involved in the cooking process. Ninja cooker cooking is a great way to simplify your life and to create the freedom and flexibility you need to live the life you want. Remember, the key to becoming a ninja grill cook is to have fun and to stay positive. Once you get started, you'll be amazed at all you can learn about cooking with your ninja grill. You can learn to cook anything on your ninja and even create your amazing recipes.

So, get started and you'll be amazed at all the fun and good food you can create!

CPSIA information can be obtained
at www.ICGtesting.com
Printed in the USA
LVHW080033050621
689455LV00020B/1147